THE GOSPEL
According to St. Luke
A PARTICIPATORY STUDY GUIDE

Geoffrey D. Lentz

Energion Publications
P. O. Box 841
Gonzalez, FL 32560

http://energionpubs.com
pubs@energion.com

ISBN-10: 1-893729-58-3
ISBN-13: 978-1-893729-58-2

LCCN: 2009928910

To
Luke Wesley,
my most excellent Theophilus.

Acknowledgments

This book is filled with the work of many different people: scholars, theologians, poets, and artists. I am grateful for their witness to the Gospel of Jesus Christ. Special thanks to the Alabama West Florida Conference of the United Methodist Church which forced me to write this study guide for an ordination requirement, to Henry Neufeld, my publisher, friend, and first Greek teacher who talked me into sharing it with others, to Wesley H. Wachob, my mentor and teacher who has inspired me to live into the Biblical text on a daily basis, and to the good people of First United Methodist Church of Pensacola who with me journey down the Emmaus road. Words fail to express my gratefulness to Elizabeth Lentz, my wife and best friend, who makes my ministry possible.

Table of Contents

Dedication..iii

Acknowledgments..iv

The Participatory Study Series..vi

Using this Book...vii

Lesson 1: Introduction and Background......................................1

Lesson 2: The Nativity and Childhood of Jesus...........................9

Lesson 3: Preparation for Ministry...19

Lesson 4: Ministry in Galilee..27

Lesson 5: The Road to Jerusalem...35

Lesson 6: Ministry in Jerusalem..41

Lesson 7: The Passion and Resurrection...................................47

Bibliography...55

Appendix A: Participatory Study Method................................57

Appendix B: Tools for Bible Study...63

The Participatory Study Series

The Participatory Study Series from Energion Publications is designed to invite Bible students to become a part of the community of faith that produced the texts we now have as scripture by studying them empathetically and with an aim to learn and grow spiritually.

The section Using this Book and the appendices are designed for the series and adapted to the particular study guide. Each author is free to emphasize different resources in the study, and individual students, group leaders, and teachers are encouraged to enhance their study through the use of additional resources.

It is our prayer at Energion Publications that each study guide will lead you deeper into scripture and more importantly closer to the One who inspired it.

– Henry Neufeld, General Editor

Using this Book

This study guide consists of three sections:

1. Introductory information
2. Study sheets
3. Appendices

I recommend that you first read the *Appendix A: Participatory Bible Study*, to learn the approach to Bible study used in this series. This guide is built around that approach. You may have other ideas, or even a completely different method, and that is fine, but it will still help if you understand the starting point. You should also have some kind of guideline for how you will approach your study. That guide is going to suggest a process of study, which I'll repeat briefly here:

1. Preparation, including materials, prayer, and opening your mind
2. Overview
3. Background
4. The inner cycle (or central loop): Meditate, Question, Research, Compare
5. Sharing

This is a study process and says very little as such about what you do in each step in the process. It is built on the principles of *lectio divina*, or "holy reading." Let's summarize those principles first and then look at the steps and see how they will help you apply these same principles.

Holy Reading: A Model for Bible Study

Lectio divina, which means holy reading, is an ancient practice of studying scripture. There are many ways to practice *lectio divina*. It has been done in many ways since Origen described it around 220 AD. The great monastic traditions of the church further developed it into distinct phases and practices. The basic principle is that reading and studying the Bible should be remarkably different than reading the morning paper or studying Shakespeare. The Bible is a sacred text; it is a *Living Word*. It should not be studied like it is dead pages from history.

When the two men were walking down the Road to Emmaus, they met the risen Christ, but did not recognize him (Luke 24). As they were walking down the road, Jesus interpreted to them all the scriptures. Only later in the breaking of the bread did they realize that Christ was with them the whole time.

Lectio Divina is a practice that, through the power of the Holy Spirit, invites the risen Christ to interpret scripture to us anew. It is a prayerful reading of scripture that expects God to speak once again through his Holy Word. Prayer should influence the way you study the Bible, and studying the Bible should influence the way you pray. In *lectio divina*, it is impossible to tell when you are studying and when you are praying. There is no difference.

This practice is usually applied on small passages of scripture for an extended period of time. However, in this study *lectio divina* is used as a strategy to study an entire book of the Bible. This is somewhat challenging because the scripture text is so large, but the prayerful approach is still crucial to Christian study of the scripture. In these lessons, the ancient practice of *lectio* is blended with modern study methods that takes into account the historical, cultural, and literary contexts.

The historical methods are important to us because they help connect us to people of a different time and place who experienced the same God that we do, learned from the same texts, and were led by the same Spirit. We do not study history because we think history is the meaning; we study history to help us meet those who wrote the texts and those who have studied the passages before us.

The lessons in this guide are designed around the four movements of *lectio divina* established by Guigo II, a 12th century Carthusian monk, in a book called *The Monk's Ladder*. He organized the practice around four rungs that help us draw closer to God through reading the Bible.

Reading (*lectio*): The first rung of the ladder is reading. Believe it or not this is the step most often skipped or diminished. It is important to do the Bible reading for each lesson in order to get the most out of it. Ideally it should be read several times so that you can become familiar with the language and themes of the text. This book is a guide to help you study the Bible. It is a supplement to the Biblical text; the text itself should have primary focus in your study. The steps of the participatory study method emphasize different ways of reading to help the text become part of you as you study.

Meditating (*meditatio*): The next thing to do is to prayerfully meditate on the text. Dig deep into it. Study the words. Break it down into pieces. In this study this is where the most of the background information is located. Look up words to find their meaning. Notice if there are any words or actions that the Holy Spirit may be leading you to examine further.

Praying (*oratio*): Third, we learn to pray the text. Use what you have learned from the scripture to formulate a prayer. It may be helpful to write it down. (There are note pages at the end of each chapter.) At the end of each lesson is a prayerful exercise that expounds on one of the themes from the text. Feel free to add your own prayers. This is where the text really becomes alive to us.

In the method used for this study guide, prayer is not seen as simply one part of the study; prayer permeates your study. You start with prayer and listening so that you will hear what God has to say through the text. Then you end by turning what you have heard from God back into prayer. The prayer never ceases!

Contemplating (*contemplatio*): The last step is the most difficult and rewarding. You have **read** the text, **studied** the text, **prayed** the text. Now it is time to **be** the text. Let it seep into your being. Be still and listen. Make sure you leave some time after the prayer for silence and reflection. It is said that Dan Rather once interviewed Mother Theresa about her prayer life. Rather asked her, "What do you say to God when you pray?". Her answer was simple; "I don't say anything; I just listen." After that he asked, "Well, what does Jesus say to you?" And Mother Theresa answered, "Oh, He doesn't say anything, either. He just listens." Listening is what is important. You may not always feel anything, but God is there.

Another facet of contemplation is to learn to *do* the text. We cannot be just hearers of the word, we must also be doers of the word. Let the scripture change the way you live you life.

Applying the Principles in Participatory Study

Preparation

As you begin the study, preparation will involve getting the materials you want to use, then prayer to begin each session of study. Part of this introductory time will be making decisions about the time and resources you can devote to this study.

This is also your time of prayer. Before you begin to read, you need to pray. Then you need to listen. You come to the text because God calls you to it.

Overview

Getting the overview is accomplished by reading Luke through at least once, but preferably three times, and in exceptional cases up to 12 times. Don't feel bad about how many times you read. Choose a number that seems reasonable to you. If you start reading the third time, and it feels like a burden, move on. This is part of *lectio* but only part. You will learn to read in other ways in different phases of your study.

Once you have read Luke through your chosen number of times, read one or two of the following

1. The entry on Luke in a Bible handbook, such as Zondervan's
2. The entry on Luke in a Bible dictionary
3. The introductory note on Luke in your study Bible
4. The introductory section of a good commentary on Luke (see Appendix B for resource details)

Here is where we introduce historical elements into your study. Don't imagine that God cannot talk to you through this text because you are so far separated from the people who wrote it. They were people like you who had hopes, dreams, gifts, and failings. Study the background to help you connect to them. Christianity is a community that extends not only in space right now but in time.

The Central Loop

For this overview, your central loop, as I call it, is your whole study of the book. Keep in mind that no element of your study is something you do just once and then forget about it. Prayer is continuous. There are multiple ways of reading, questioning, studying, and sharing.

For study, I have divided the Gospel of Luke into seven units in chronological order for study.

Introduction and Background (Luke 1:1-4)

The Nativity and Childhood of Jesus (Luke 1:5-2:52)

Preparation for Ministry (Luke 3:1-4:30)

Ministry in Galilee (Luke 4:31-9:50)

The Road to Jerusalem (9:51-19:27)

Ministry in Jerusalem (19:28-21:38)

The Passion and Resurrection (22:1-24:53)

This is a false division: Luke was meant to be read and understood holistically. It is important to keep the whole Gospel of Luke (and even the Acts of the Apostles) in your mind as you study a particular unit. You can choose to read either just the suggested passages, and put them in context by memory from your earlier overview, or you can read through the entire book again with each unit, concentrating on the passages that emphasize that particular topic.

This is most closely related to *meditatio*, but the implementation of *meditatio* extends into the next section where you question the text in a directed way. Don't concentrate on the boundaries between one activity and the next. They are all related!

With each topic there will be an opportunity to try to think of new questions one might ask for further study. Generating new questions helps keep us from getting stale. Not only do I not have all the answers; I don't even have all the questions!

Think of a question primarily as a way to prepare your mind to hear the text. When we listen or read, we often hear what we expect to hear. If I'm listening to the radio for weather, I may miss a major discussion of politics. You can miss what God is saying to you through a Bible writer because you are looking for something else. Questioning is thus an important part of *meditatio*, but it also relates closely to *oratio*—take your questions to God in prayer.

Finally, find something to share. Remember that sharing can be in the form of a question. For example, one might ask others how they understand a particular word, such as "incarnation," "poverty," or "atonement." Take notes on their answers, and bring that information back to your study.

Then ask yourself what your neighbors will hear when you make particular statements, such as "I must be bold for Jesus!" or "Jesus is the only way to receive atonement." Do those statements mean something to them? Do they mean the same thing to them as they do to you?

This is part of *contemplatio*, as you try to be and do the text. We often think of sharing primarily as telling someone things that we have learned. But if what you learned is that God loves prisoners, for example, you might find that the best way of sharing that lesson is to become active in prison ministry.

Sharing demonstrates that you don't believe the text is your private possession. It is God's gift to the Christian community.

Resources

The following resources are referenced regularly in the text. In a small group it is a good idea to have different members of the group bring different references. For individual study, use a selection:

1. Study Bibles, with particular reference to *The Learning Bible*, the *New Interpreter's Study Bible*, and The *Today's New International Version (TNIV) Study Bible*. These are not the only Bibles I recommend using, but they do represent a range of versions and viewpoints, and I will note specific articles from each one. You can look for similar articles in your study Bible. I don't use resources from any one perspective. Look at materials you are likely to disagree with in order to stimulate your thinking. (See Appendix B for information on these resources. The Participatory Bible Study web site, http://www.deepbiblestudy.com, is regularly updated with ideas about materials. For specific materials on Luke, see http://lukestudy.com.)

2. Concordances, either English only, or those that include material on the original languages. If you get a concordance, find one that is based on the Bible version you use.
3. Bible Dictionaries, which overlap Study Bibles and Bible Handbooks in terms of their use, but which are very useful for general study of topics you may find.
4. Bible Handbooks, used in much the same way as study Bibles, but without the text of the Bible itself included.

When it comes to comparing passages you will find your study Bible, concordance, and any Bible with reference notes to be very useful. Remember, however, that even the cross-references are just someone's opinion of how one passage is related to another. You don't have to agree. Look at the passages yourself, and ask not just whether they are related, but *how* they are related.

Remember to keep an open mind and a receptive heart while studying the Bible. Study prayerfully. Meditate on what you read. Try to place yourself in the audience of people who might have first heard this book read to them aloud in a small house church.

The following pamphlets in the Participatory Study Series from Energion Publications may also be helpful in your study:

✔ What's in a Version?
✔ The Authority of the Bible
✔ What about the KJV?
✔ What is Biblical Criticism?
✔ I Want to Pray
✔ Understanding the Search for the Historical Jesus

You can find these free in various formats online at http://www.participatorystudyseries.com.

Lesson 1: Introduction and Background

Objective: At the end of this session, the class will have a basic understanding of the setting, context, authorship, and other background enabling them to see the text as a whole with distinct Lukan emphases.

Opening Prayer: Lord, open our hearts and minds by the power of your Holy Spirit, that, as the Scriptures are read and your Word proclaimed, we may hear with joy what you say to us today. Amen. (A prayer of illumination from the Reformed tradition)

Reading: Luke 1:1-4

Read an introduction to Luke in the study Bible of your choice.

Review an outline of Luke in any or all of the recommended Study Bibles

Lesson:

What Do We Know of Luke from the Bible?

He was a well-educated Greek speaker. He is the best story teller in the New Testament. He is known for giving us many interesting details. He weaves stories, songs, and sermons together in elaborate ways in order to most effectively tell other people about Jesus.

He was not an eye-witness to Jesus' life, but documented an account from "eyewitnesses" and "servants of the word". He drew on the Gospel of Mark and other written and oral sources (maybe an unknown source that Matthew also used; scholars call Q).

He was, most likely, a Gentile that converted to Judaism before becoming a follower of Jesus.

He was, probably a traveling companion of Paul (see Philemon 24; II Timothy 4:11). In Luke's second volume of work, the Acts of the Apostles, sometimes the language shifts to the use of "we" indicating that he was on the missionary journey (Acts 16, 20, 21, and 27).

What Do We Know of Luke Through Church Tradition?

Because of his attention to detail and high level of education, he may have been a physician (see Colossians 4:14). Some tradition says that he was an artist, even painting the first picture of the Virgin Mary. Each of the gospel writers paints a picture of Jesus in his gospel that is distinct; just like different artists will paint the same person in different ways capturing different qualities that appealed to the artist. As you read through Luke notice the things that Luke focuses on and the subtle and not so subtle difference between this gospel and the other three.

Eusebius of Caesarea (c. 275 – 339), said that Luke was a Syrian from Antioch.

He is considered the patron saint of people in the medical field and artists.

Why Was the Gospel Written?

The Acts of the Apostles (Luke's second volume) ties the ministry of Jesus to the activity of the Holy Spirit in the ministry of the apostles, particularly Paul. Because of Luke's close relationship to Paul it is thought that he was writing for the churches Paul founded in order to give them greater understanding of the life and ministry of Jesus.

Some see the gospel as an apologetic to leaders of the Greco-Roman world, maybe even intended for those in Rome. Limiting the scope of the gospel to just a Lukan community misses the point that gospels are open texts designed to impact wide audiences. Gospels were intended to have wide circulation among the churches.

When was it written?

Most scholars date the Gospel between 80 AD and 100 AD. Because of the significant reliance on Mark it could not be much earlier than 80. If it had been later than 100 AD it may have begun to display the developing church structure found in the later Epistles.

The Prologue (1:1-4)

It is clear from the first verse that there were other known accounts of Jesus' life. Therefore Luke's use of a framework from Mark is understandable as well as the content from other sources.

Luke wants to make it clear to his readers that his account is not the first, but it is derived from careful research from eyewitness testimony and is an "orderly account".

We do not know much about Theophilus, the recipient of the Gospel. He probably was a church leader. Many have noted that Theophilus means, "lover of God." Maybe Luke intended the double meaning. All who love God may come to learn the truth about Jesus, and in some way this gospel is addressed to us.

Discussion Questions:

1. How does knowing that Luke used several sources to write his gospel affect the way you think about scripture? How do sources from "eye-witnesses" and sources from "preachers" differ?
2. Luke has a somewhat different way of stating the thrust of the gospel with several distinct emphases. Use a

study Bible or the Internet to make a list of major themes in Luke's gospel.

3. Luke became the patron saint for artists because of his artistic use of language and poetry. Why do you think Luke includes so many songs and poems in his gospel?

4. Some have tried to study scripture isolated from the spiritual life of the church searching for "historical and literary" value divorced from theology and prayer (see preface chapter). How does reading the gospel as a "God lover" (Theophilus) differ from reading the gospel from a non-Christian perspective? What is the difference between reading holy scripture or reading the daily newspaper?

> **Exercise:** Compare the uses of parables in Matthew, Mark, and Luke using the table in the *TNIV Study Bible*, pg. 1752. Notice the shared parables and the number of parables that are only in Luke.

Reflection:

Pray the song of Zechariah together. You may want to read it responsively together. What words and images speak to you?

The Song of Zechariah (Translation from Common Worship)

Blessed be the Lord the God of Israel
who has come to His people and set them free.
He has raised up for us a mighty Saviour,
born of the house of His servant David.
Through His holy prophets God promised of old
to save us from our enemies, from the hands of all that
hate us,
To show mercy to our ancestors,
and to remember His holy covenant.
This was the oath God swore to our father Abraham:

to set us free from the hands of our enemies,
Free to worship Him without fear,
holy and righteous in His sight all the days of our life.
And you, child, shall be called the prophet of the Most High,
for you will go before the Lord to prepare His way,
To give His people knowledge of salvation
by the forgiveness of all their sins.
In the tender compassion of our God
the dawn from on high shall break upon us,
To shine on those who dwell in darkness and the shadow of
   death,
and to guide our feet into the way of peace.

Reflection 2

Review the picture of Saint Luke's bull on the next page. The symbols for the four evangelists are taken from Ezekiel's vision of God's throne. There were four living creatures each with four faces: human, lion, ox, and eagle. Luke's gospel begins and ends with the Temple therefore the symbol chosen for him is the ox or bull. What other reasons can you think of for the bull being chosen? Why is the ox standing or adorned with a halo in the picture?

Closing Prayer

Have members of the group share about occasions in their lives when they waited in expectation. Ask them what they expect to learn from studying the Gospel of Luke. Close in prayer asking God to meet you in the text as you study the Gospel of Luke together.

Notes

_____

_____

_____

_____

_____

_____

_____

_____

_____

_____

_____

_____

_____

_____

_____

Notes

_____

_____

_____

_____

_____

_____

_____

_____

_____

_____

_____

_____

_____

_____

Lesson 2: The Nativity and Childhood of Jesus

Objective: At the end of this session, the class will have a better understanding of the significance of Jesus' birth and how the events surrounding it apply to the liturgical calendar and their salvation.

Opening Prayer:

O God, who looked on us when we had fallen down into death, and resolved to redeem us by the Advent of your only begotten Son; grant, we beg you, that those who confess his glorious Incarnation may also be admitted to the fellowship of their Redeemer, through the same Jesus Christ our Lord.

–St. Ambrose

Reading: Luke 1:5-2:52; 1 Samuel 1

Lesson:

Zechariah and Elizabeth

The story of Jesus begins and ends in the Temple. This highlights the continuity of the gospel with the history of Israel. Jesus' birth echoes the foretold births of Ishmael (Gen 16:7-13), Isaac (Gen 17:1-21, 18:1-15), and Samson (Judges 13:2-33). The story Elizabeth and Zechariah echo the story of Abraham and Sarah (Gen 16 and 18), Isaac and Rebecca (Gen 25), and Elkanah and Hannah (1 Sam 1). Luke ensures that we know that the Old Testament scriptures dovetail perfectly with the story of Jesus.

Zechariah's Temple Service

At the temple, priests were divided into 24 groups, and offerings would be offered twice a day; one on the inside altar and one on the outside altar. Two priests from scheduled groups where chosen to bring the offering. The honor of offering the sacrifice in the temple usually came only once in a lifetime. It was while Zechariah was carrying out his liturgical duties that God interrupted him. After the offering, the priest would pronounce a blessing on the people, but Zechariah was unable to speak. His once in a lifetime opportunity was ruined because God was beginning a new thing.

Angel Announcements

The Gospel of Luke is filled with angelic announcements. The word *angel* means messenger or one who brings news. The root for *angel* is in the word evangelism (sharing good news). All of the angelic announcements follow a similar pattern. After the angel appears, the person being visited is filled with fear. The angel then brings a word of good news. In Tobit (in the Apocrypha), an angel appears to a betrothed woman and kills her husband. With this cultural background, it makes sense that she would be afraid. People are always afraid when they encounter angels. These are not the angels on our Christmas cards. They are strong terrifying warriors, but they bring messages of good news.

The Annunciation

This is the traditional title of the moment when the incarnation began. Here the angel delivers another message. It tells of a greater miracle than Zechariah's moment in the temple six months earlier. "The Lord is with you," is the announcement that the angel makes. This message is similar to the message that Jesus is Emmanuel, "God with us" (Matthew 1:23).

God chooses Mary because she is "full of grace", not because of anything that she has done. God chose Mary, not because she deserved this honor or that we deserved the honor, but just because of God's favor. She has been the main role model or template in Christian tradition for receiving Christ and becoming a Christian. Her statement "Let it be done unto me according to your word" is called her fiat. This is where Christians begin their journeys of faith.

The Incarnation

Christianity proclaims that God became flesh (John 1). The early church saw the annunciation as the starting point for the incarnation. The church celebrated this day of the Annunciation before Christmas was celebrated. Scholars say that the church started with a uni-feast that celebrated the life, death, and resurrection at Easter (Passover). This uni-feast also included the Annunciation (traditionally March 25). When the calendar began to be expanded, the date of Jesus' birth was placed nine months after the Annunciation on Christmas (December 25).

Despite the fact that the full doctrine of the Trinity is not described in detail in scripture, we can nevertheless see the Trinity at work in some of the most important scenes in the gospels. In the Annunciation, the Holy Spirit of the Father came upon Mary who was to give birth to the Son. This Trinitarian theme reappears in other moments of revelation including the Baptism of Christ and the Transfiguration.

John to Jesus

John the Baptist stands as a link from Israel's history to the life of Jesus. He fills the role of an Old Testament prophet. His purpose is to point toward Jesus as the Messiah. The church has celebrated John the Baptist's birth six months from Jesus' birth like Luke states (June 24). These dates also have meteorological

signification. Jesus' conception coincides with the vernal
equinox, his birth with the winter solstice. Where John's birth
coincides with the summer solstice. The church believed that
this celebration of light illustrates graphically John's message
"you must increase and I must decrease" (John 3:30).

Mary's Song

Mary's song to God
her savior is important
because that is what
Jesus means, "God
saves". Her song, the
Magnificat, expresses the
dramatic reversal or reset

> **Exercise**: For more background
> on the Magnificat read the *New
> Interpreter's Study Bible* notes on
> 1:46-55 pgs.1853-1854.

of the world. As we will see in future weeks, this theme of
reversal is integral to Luke's Gospel. Mary's song begins to
prepare the hearer for the radical nature of the Gospel. Her
song is structured similarly to 1 Samuel 2:1-10 linking the
Messianic references of kings to Jesus.

Women in Luke

There is a unique role that women play in the Gospel of
Luke. More than any other New Testament writer Luke tells the
story of many women. The most profound of these stories is
of Mary the mother of Jesus. Luke also tells of female disciples
that followed Jesus in the eighth chapter. Women also play a
major role in the resurrection.

The Nativity

The radical reversal of the Magnificat is carried on in the
Christmas story. The first two verses, referring to Caesar
Augustus and Quirinius, set the backdrop for the story.
Augustus was labeled as the "bringer of peace" in his day, but
Luke sets Jesus as the true bringer of peace. Jesus' kingdom

brings an end to Caesar's. Shepherds have two roles in the story. They tie Jesus to David in Bethlehem, who was a lowly shepherd, and show

> **Exercise:** In the *Learning Bible* on p.1870, read the cultural background of Shepherds in Bible times.

God's care for the outcast by picking up Luke's theme of gospel reversal. It is the shepherds, not Caesar, who are invited to the birth of the new Davidic king.

Presentation and Circumcision

These two stories continue the temple theme and tie Jesus to Israel's history and law. Jesus is raised as a Jew following all the Jewish law.

Discussion Questions:

1. Zechariah was going through the motions of the liturgy and God showed up. Has that ever happened to you? Have you ever experienced God unexpectedly at church or on your own?
2. In what ways is our own salvation experience similar to Mary's experience of grace at the Annunciation? How can Mary's experience enhance our own spiritual lives?
3. What are the pros and cons of celebrating Christmas and other holidays in the church year?
4. How can our lives be more like John the Baptist's ministry and point to Christ?
5. How do African American Spirituals like "Go Down Moses" and "Mary Don't You Weep" compare to Mary's song (Luke 1:46-55)? How are they similar as well as different?
6. The Christmas story is very familiar to us. Was there anything that jumped out at you in a different way during this recent reading?

7. Luke's gospel shows that God has an interest in those
    that are on the lowest levels of society. This is a radically
    different politic than that of our world. In what ways
    does the gospel politic, if adopted by Christians,
    challenge the existing social structures?

Reflection: Read or sing together the great Christmas hymn by
Charles Wesley, "Hark the Herald Angels Sing". The lyrics to
this song are some of the clearest and most complete theological
statements on the incarnation of Christ.

Hark the herald angels sing
"Glory to the newborn King!
Peace on earth and mercy mild
God and sinners reconciled"
Joyful, all ye nations rise
Join the triumph of the skies
With the angelic host proclaim:
"Christ is born in Bethlehem"
Hark! The herald angels sing
"Glory to the newborn King!"

Christ by highest heav'n adored
Christ the everlasting Lord!
Late in time behold Him come
Offspring of a Virgin's womb
Veiled in flesh the Godhead see
Hail the incarnate Deity
Pleased as man with man to dwell
Jesus, our Emmanuel
Hark! The herald angels sing
"Glory to the newborn King!"

Hail the heav'n-born Prince of Peace!
Hail the Son of Righteousness!

Light and life to all He brings
Ris'n with healing in His wings
Mild He lays His glory by
Born that man no more may die
Born to raise the sons of earth
Born to give them second birth
Hark! The herald angels sing
"Glory to the newborn King!"

Reflection 2:

Have the class view the Icon of Luke painting, the Madonna and Child. Why do you think that Luke felt like his gospel needed a fuller account of Mary's life and relationship to Jesus? Why is this an important part of the gospel?

Closing Prayer:

St. Ignatius of Loyola developed a way of praying that heavily uses imagery. It is particularly helpful in today's image driven society. One of the spiritual practices that he taught was to focus on the Annunciation. This practice is formatted on a triptych, or three-panel painting.

First, think about the great need the world has for God. Bring images to your mind of war, sickness, famine, and disaster. Also, think about and visualize your own need.

Second, think about the goodness and nature of God. Try to think of some way to picture his grace by dwelling on the cross and the eternal love of God.

Last, imagine these two images meeting, where the grace and presence of God converges with the needs of the world. Visualize the Annunciation as the angel tells Mary that she is to bear the Son of God. Let Christ be present in your life like in Mary's. Focus on how Christ is present in your needs and the needs of the world.

Notes

Lesson 3: Preparation for Ministry

Objective: At the end of this session, the class will understand two major thrusts of Luke's gospel: the Jubilee theme and the identity of Jesus as God's Son. They will be able to apply this to their lives through the practice of forgiveness and remembering their baptisms.

Opening Prayer: Almighty God, who by our baptism into the death and resurrection of thy Son Jesus Christ dost turn us from the old life of sin: Grant that we, being reborn to new life in him, may live in righteousness and holiness all our days; through the same thy Son Jesus Christ our Lord, who liveth and reigneth with thee and the Holy Spirit, one God, now and for ever. Amen.   – The Book of Common Prayer

Reading: Luke 3:1-4:30; Isaiah 58; Leviticus 25

Lesson:

The Significance of John the Baptist

✔ In Chapter 3, Luke sets the date of the beginning of John the Baptist's ministry against the imperial, political, and priestly offices. This shows that the gospel will be far reaching.

✔ John the Baptist is described as an Old Testament prophet with the phrase "the word of God came" (Jeremiah 1:1-5; Isaiah 6:1; Ezekiel 1:1-3) and the use of Isaiah 40.

✔ Luke contains the fullest account of John the Baptist. He warns of coming judgment, calls for social and ethical reforms, and announces the coming Messiah. John's message on social reforms prefigures the main thrust of the gospel in Luke. The warning about the stones (3:7) reverses the text from Isaiah 51:1-2 and sets the stage for the gospel to include Gentiles.

✔ Fire (3:9) prefigures the fire of Pentecost in Acts and the refiner's fire.

✔ The purpose of John in Luke's gospel is to point to Jesus as God's Son.

The Baptism of the Lord

✔ Luke does not record the actual baptism, but the prayer that follows. This emphasizes the importance of prayer, and prefigures the embodiment of the Holy Spirit at Pentecost.

✔ This baptismal scene has been important for the church because the full Trinity is present in the voice of the Father, the decent of a dove (Holy Spirit) onto the Son with whom God is well-pleased.

> **Exercise**: Read the *Learning Bible's* description of Baptism on pg. 1874

✔ It culminates the proclamation that Jesus is God's Son that began in the Nativity story and was proclaimed by the 12 year-old Jesus.

✔ The genealogy (3:23-38) records Jesus' age and further designates him as God's Son. The words "as thought" reveal that Luke knows that this is not his real genealogy, but nevertheless he desires to trace his family back to God. This places Jesus as a new Adam, the beginning of new creation, but also places the focus on being God's Son. It relates Jesus to the history of Israel.

The Temptation

✔ This story serves to describe different ways for Jesus to live out his divine sonship.

✔ The order of events is different than in Matthew. The final temptation in Luke is at the temple; this highlights Luke's use of the temple.

✔ The first is a temptation to exploit his sonship for his own use.

✔ The Greek use of if in the temptation (first class conditional) means since. The devil already knows Jesus' nature so he says, "since you are the Son of God".

✔ The second temptation is to gain power through compromise. This is the easy way out.

✔ The third temptation is set at the temple. It foreshadows Jesus' future choice to do his Father's will and face death in Jerusalem. His true sonship would be lived out not by avoiding death, but by facing it on the cross.

✔ The devil leaves until an opportune time at Jesus' death (see 22:3, 31, 53). It is rejection of the cross which is final temptation.

✔ Jesus leaves the temptation filled with the power of the Spirit to do ministry in Galilee.

The Program of Jesus' Ministry and His Rejection at Nazareth

✔ This story is the first ministry and teaching experience recorded in the gospel. Most scholars see this incident as a summary of the focus of Jesus'

> **Exercise:** Look up the words *forgiveness* and *Jubilee* in a Bible dictionary.

ministry. Jesus read from the scroll of Isaiah, highlighting the 58th chapter. This sets the program for Jesus' ministry in the gospel of Luke.

✔ The text from Isaiah refers to the Jubilee year. The Jubilee was required by the law in Leviticus 25. It was a radical reset of society where debts where forgiven, slaves were released, and all land went back to its original owners. It is clear in Luke that the Jubilee is central to the gospel and kingdom of Jesus Christ. Jesus is consistently speaking of radical forgiveness and transformation in society. You can follow this jubilee theme from Mary's song, the angelic visitation to the shepherds, the Sermon on the Plain, all the way to the great commission in Luke.

✔ The first major ministry experience in Luke was a failure. In fact, they tried to kill him. Preaching this radical gospel of forgiveness is very challenging and it did eventually have him killed.

Discussion Questions:

1. In what ways are our baptisms similar to Christ's baptism? And in what ways are they different?

2. After the baptism, the Spirit led Jesus into the wilderness to be tempted. How does God's Spirit challenge our assumptions about where Jesus might lead us?

3. Jesus used the comforting words of scripture to combat the Devil's temptations. What are some scripture verses or stories that you cling to in times of trial and temptation?

4. The first recorded ministry experience of Jesus was a failure. How does that change the expectations that you have on the ministry to which God has called you?

5. Luke highlights the radical nature of the Gospel by frequently using Jubilee year imagery. In what ways does this radical reset offer you comfort, and in what ways does it make you uncomfortable?

Reflection: Have the class review the picture of   the Isenheim Altar Frontal of St. John the Baptist from the Isenheim Altarpiece circa 1512-16, by Matthias Grünewald. Why do you think John is depicted with such an elongated finger?

Closing Prayer:

Recite the Apostles Creed together. This creed was developed to prepare candidates for baptism. As you recite the creed together, reaffirm your baptismal vows, and strengthen your identity in Christ as God's children.

I believe in God, the Father Almighty,
    the Maker of heaven and earth,
    and in Jesus Christ, His only Son, our Lord:
Who was conceived by the Holy Ghost,
    born of the virgin Mary,
    suffered under Pontius Pilate,
    was crucified, dead, and buried;
He descended into hell.
The third day He arose again from the dead;
He ascended into heaven,
    and sitteth on the right hand of God the Father Almighty;
    from thence he shall come to judge the quick and the
  dead.
I believe in the Holy Ghost;
    the holy catholic church;
    the communion of saints;
    the forgiveness of sins;
    the resurrection of the body;
    and the life everlasting.
Amen.

Notes

Notes

Lesson 4: Ministry in Galilee

Objective: At the end of this session, the class will have a basic understanding of Jesus' healing ministry and be able to identify how they have experienced Christ's healing and salvation. They also will be challenged by Jesus' teachings of radical forgiveness.

Opening Prayer:

> Loving God, close your eyes to our sins....
> Make us whole, steadfast in spirit.
> Broken are our bones, yet you can heal us
> and we shall leap for joy and dance again. Amen
>   -Jim Cotter

Reading: Luke 4:31-9:50; Matthew 5:1-7:28.

Lesson:

Jesus Starts his Ministry in Galilee

✔ After his rejection in Nazareth, Jesus' ministry extends to Galilee. In this area of the text there are multiple healings. Even the exorcisms are part of his healing ministry. God desires

> **Exercise:** Review the map of Galilee in the *Learning Bible* pg. 1879 for a better understanding of the region of Galilee.

wholeness in body, mind, and spirit. It is interesting to note that the demons always know the true nature of Jesus, even though it takes awhile for the disciples to learn of it.

✔ Most of the healing stories focus on the faith of the person being healed, but it is interesting to note in the healing of the paralytic Jesus healed the man when he saw the faith of his friends. The gospel is more that just a private affair. It involves the whole community.

Jesus Calls His Disciples

✔ Peter, James, and John were fishing when Christ called them to "catch people." The life of a disciple is clearly outwardly focused.   Every Christian is called to be an evangelist (sharers of the good news).   They dropped everything to follow him.

✔ In chapter 6, Jesus calls all twelve of the disciples. And later in chapter 9, Jesus sends the disciples out to proclaim the kingdom of God. But before they go, he equips them with the power and authority to do ministry.

Controversies with the Pharisees

In this section of Luke, there are five controversies in which the Pharisees play a major role (the healing of the paralytic, the call of Levi, the permissibility of fasting, picking grain on the Sabbath, and healing on the Sabbath).   Many of these controversies recognize the importance of the old covenant. The old is not dismantled because of the new, but reinterpreted and strengthened.

Jesus' Teaching and the Sermon on the Plain

Luke's Sermon on the Plain (see 4:17) closely mirrors Matthew's Sermon on the Mount. This is the main recording of Jesus' teaching ministry.   The

Exercise: For more background on the *Sermon on the Plain* read the notes on 6:20-49 in the *New Interpreter's Study Bible*, pg. 1864-1865.

Sermon on the Plain differs from Matthew's in that it has a

grouping of "woes" to match the "beatitudes". This clearly matches the program of ministry developed in chapter 4 and in the Magnificat. There also is a greater focus on forgiveness, expanding the Jubilee theme already established.

Miracles and Parables that Illustrate Jesus' Power and Identity

✔ The next major section of text (7-9:50) deals with the identity of Jesus. The story of the centurion illustrates Jesus as a "man of authority". The story of the widow's son paints Jesus as a prophet in the line of Elijah. The messengers from John the Baptist are interested to know if Jesus is the Messiah. Jesus' special identity is clearly displayed when he calms the storm. They ask (8:25), "who then is this, that he commands over the winds and the water, and they obey him?"

✔ This unit culminates with Simon Peter's great confession that Jesus is "the Messiah of God." It is after all this, that the Transfiguration takes place. This scene parallels the baptism, as Jesus' identity as God's Son is proclaimed from the heavens. Moses and Elijah serve as representatives of the Law and the Prophets (encapsulating the whole history of Israel) testifying of Jesus' true divine identity. The early church saw the image of the Holy Trinity present in this like in the Annunciation and Baptism of the Lord. The Holy Spirit is conveyed by the great cloud surrounding the Son, with the voice of the Father echoing through the heavens. Jesus is greater than any prophet. He is the very Son of God.

Discussion Questions:

1. The Greek word *sozo*, refers to salvation and healing in the New Testament. In what ways have you experienced the healing powers of Christ physically, mentally, or spiritually? In what ways does the community of faith

help bring an individual to salvation and healing (like the paralytic's friends)?

2. When Jesus sent out the twelve he also equipped them with the power and authority to do the work of the gospel. In what ways has God equipped you to perform the tasks to which God has called you?

3. The message of the Sermon on the Plain is even more radical in many ways than the Sermon on the Mount. How does this great sermon of Jesus challenge your way of living? How might we be able to not just hear these words, but act on them (6:46-49)?

4. It took awhile for the disciples to know Jesus' true nature. After many twists and turns in the narrative, Peter was finally able to confess Jesus as Messiah and then Jesus was revealed in divine glory in the Transfiguration. Can you describe a moment in time when God's nature was revealed to you in a special way?

Reflection: Sing or read together the great Charles Wesley tune "Love Divine All Loves Excelling". Think of how the words challenge us to live out Jesus' radical teaching of love and forgiveness. End with a moment of silence to allow God time to speak and be present to the group.

Love divine, all loves excelling,
Joy of heaven to earth come down;
Fix in us thy humble dwelling;
All thy faithful mercies crown!
Jesus, Thou art all compassion,
Pure unbounded love Thou art;
Visit us with Thy salvation;
Enter every trembling heart.

Breathe, O breathe Thy loving Spirit,
Into every troubled breast!
Let us all in Thee inherit;

Let us find that second rest.
Take away our bent to sinning;
Alpha and Omega be;
End of faith, as its Beginning,
Set our hearts at liberty.

Come, Almighty to deliver,
Let us all Thy life receive;
Suddenly return and never,
Never more Thy temples leave.
Thee we would be always blessing,
Serve Thee as Thy hosts above,
Pray and praise Thee without ceasing,
Glory in Thy perfect love.

Finish, then, Thy new creation;
Pure and spotless let us be.
Let us see Thy great salvation
Perfectly restored in Thee;
Changed from glory into glory,
'Til in heaven we take our place,
'Til we cast our crowns before Thee,
Lost in wonder, love, and praise.

Reflection 2:   Review the Icon of the Healing of the
Paralytic. The paralytic was unable to come to Jesus on his own,
so his friends brought him. In the image the crowd is pushed
back and room is made, how can we make room for people who
are in need to find healing and wholeness in our communities
and churches?

Closing Prayer:

Ask members of the group to pray short prayers or sentences that give thanks for what God is doing in their lives. Invite them to create a prayer that is related to one of the themes from the lesson.

Notes

_____

_____

_____

_____

_____

_____

_____

_____

_____

_____

_____

_____

_____

_____

Notes

Lesson 5: The Road to Jerusalem

Objective: At the end of this session, the class will learn about Jesus' journey to the cross, and apply this cruciform journey to their own walk with God as we learn about loving God and neighbor.

Opening Prayer:

Lord, I know
that one of the best ways I can show
my love for you
is by loving other people.
Sometimes this is easy—when I'm with people I like—
Please help me when loving is hard,
when people are unkind,
when they don't understand,
when I just don't like them.
Teach me to love as you loved
when you were walking about in Palestine—
Teach me to love as you love now—
Everyone
Always

-Brother Kenneth and Sister Geraldine

Reading: Luke 9:51-19:27

Lesson:

Journey to Jerusalem

This entire section is on the journey to Jerusalem. In 9:51, it comes near for the time for Jesus "to be taken up" and Jesus sets his face toward Jerusalem. To be "taken up" literally reads as his "exodus". This begins a long journey to his death. All of the parables, miracles, and teachings in this section are permeated with this knowledge. The three mentions of Jerusalem before his arrival outline this text into three sections and punctuate the journey with deep emotions. The journey is particularly stressful to Jesus. In 12:49-53, is a great description of how the journey to the cross changes the tone of Jesus' ministry. He says, " I have a baptism with which to be baptized, and what stress I am under until it is completed!" Also, the lament over Jerusalem in 13:31-35 is particularly moving—"a city that kills the prophets". Jesus says that he longs to gather it like a mother hen gathers her brood.

The Greatest Commandment

On the journey a lawyer asked Jesus how to inherit eternal life. Jesus does not answer his question, but instead asks him to answer it. Then the lawyer summarizes the basic thrust of the gospel: to love God and neighbor. But Jesus reminds us that it is not knowing the right answers that bring life but doing it.

To illustrate this dual thrust of the gospel, Luke joins two stories- first, the story of the Good Samaritan to illustrate love of neighbor, and second, the story of Mary and Martha to illustrate love of God and worship of Jesus. These two stories function as a diptych (two pictures that interpret each other). The story of the Good Samaritan is about doing the work of helping others, while the complimentary story of Mary and Martha is about not doing, but worshiping. They do not contradict each other, but in fact, in a mysterious way, are the same.

Exercise: For background on the Lord's Prayer and Jesus' use of "Father" refer to the *New Interpreter's Study Bible* note on Luke 11:1-13.

Prayer

Prayer is a major theme in the Gospel of Luke. In this Gospel we find Jesus praying more often that the other synoptic gospels. In chapter 11, we find Jesus praying in his usual place. His disciples want to learn to pray the way that he prayed. Jesus then does not really answer their question on how to pray, but instead focuses on the more important matter—to whom we pray. He defines God as Father. The parables that follow define God as generous as a friend and as loving as a father. He then ends with a promise that the Father will generously give the Holy Spirit to those who ask.

Hospitality

In the Gospel of Luke, eating and hospitality play a major role. Jesus is always feasting with sinners or inviting outcasts to a banquet. Feasting is a symbol of kingdom hospitality. In 14:7-14, Jesus instructs us to invite the poor, the lame, and the blind to our banquet. This combines Luke's Jubilee reversal motif with the theme of feasting. The parable of the Great Dinner is similar (14:15-24). Their guests are brought in from the "highway and byways" to attend the banquet. God's feast is for everyone. This is further developed at the Last Supper and the feast on the Road to Emmaus. This hospitality includes all those on the bottom of society, especially children (18:15-17).

The "Lost" Parables

There is a string of three "lost parables". None of these parables are really focused on the lost subjects, but on the one that does the finding. The parable of the lost coin and the lost sheep portray God as an obsessive seeker of the lost. This continues the hospitality theme already developed. In the story commonly called the "prodigal son", the focus is on God as a father that is wasteful (prodigal) in his love, not the wasteful son.

The Coming of the Kingdom

Many of the stories on the road to Jerusalem have the theme of the coming kingdom. As Jesus draws closer to Jerusalem the focus on God's realm becomes more important. The parable of the rich man and Lazarus (16:19-31) continues the theme of Jubilee reversal in a kingdom perspective. Jesus' long kingdom teaching in 17: 20-37 proclaims that the "kingdom of God is among you". This is a powerful proclamation and seems, at least in part, to proclaim his own presence.

Discussion Questions:

1. In what ways does the Christian life mirror Jesus' journey to Jerusalem?
2. How are love of God and love of neighbor complimentary to one another?
3. Often the church has a very limited definition of hospitality—linking it to southern living, iced tea, coffee, and handshakes. How does the radical nature of Jesus' gospel give new meaning to hospitality and the church's practice of it?
4. The story of the "prodigal son" is not about us finding God, but about God finding us. How does this change our view of salvation? Why do you think we have the tendency to turn the Bible into a story about us finding God rather than, the true thrust of the gospel, God finding us?

Reflection: On the next page is a picture of the Sander's Family Window at First United Methodist Church, Pensacola, circa 1910. It places the story of Mary and Martha next to the story of the Good Samaritan. How do these stories interpret each other in light of the dual command to love God and neighbor?

Closing Prayer:

Make a list of people or groups of people that are often not welcomed in our homes and our churches. Close by praying for them and praying that God can teach us to reach out to these people. End with the Lord's Prayer.

Notes

Lesson 6: Ministry in Jerusalem

Objective: At the end of this session, the class will have a basic understanding of the factors that lead to Jesus' death in Jerusalem, of the general resurrection, and of the Second Coming of Christ.

Opening Prayer:

Lord Jesus,
When you rode into Jerusalem on Palm Sunday,
You knew it was the road to the cross,
Yet you still took that road.
Give me the courage to take the road I should today,
whatever it may mean, wherever it may lead.
May I travel trustfully and obediently through this day,
content to leave tomorrow in your safe hands,
and tonight rest in your peace.
-Margaret Cundiff

Reading: Luke 19:28-21:38

Lesson:

Entry into Jerusalem

Jesus entered Jerusalem riding on a donkey; the long journey to the cross is over. The end had begun. Jesus is welcomed with loud cries, but he weeps again over the city. His first action is to cleanse the temple and the leaders begin to look for a way to kill him. In 21:37-38, it says that during this time Jesus was teaching in the temple every day and would spent each night on

> **Exercise:** For more background on the cleansing of the temple read the notes on Luke 19:45-48 in the *New Interpreter's Study Bible*, p. 1891.

the Mount of Olives. All the people would get up early in the morning to listen to him teach. The temple is the setting for these teachings that follow. It is particularly clear with the story of the widow's offering that Jesus is at the temple. The gospel of Luke starts at the temple and it also ends at the temple. This ties Jesus' ministry to the history of Israel and the sacrificial system of the temple.

The parable of the wicked tenants is a micro-gospel. It lays out in story form his own death. It also shows how his death is a stumbling block for many, but it is the cornerstone on which the kingdom is built. It infuriated the leaders so much that they wanted to kill him that very hour.

Questioned by the Scribes, Pharisees, and Sadducees

In 20:20-26, the scribes and the priests have sent spies to trip up Jesus on his radical political views. They ask Jesus about paying taxes. His answer is "give unto Caesar the things that are Caesar's and unto God the things that are God's". If he answered pay your taxes, the people would have been upset in his support of the empire and he would have undercut his political message. If he had told them not to pay taxes, then the people would have been pleased, but he would have been brought up on political charges. His answer is well crafted. Yes, the denarius has Caesar face imprinted on it, but all of humanity has God's image on it. In reality nothing really belongs to Caesar, but the "whole earth is the Lord's and all that dwell therein."

Jesus is also questioned about his teaching of the resurrection. Here Jesus foreshadows his resurrection and also the general resurrection. Many Jewish leaders were looking for the Resurrection at the end of the age. It was to be a sign of God's victory. Christians

> **Exercise:** Look up resurrection in a Bible dictionary.

maintain this belief in "resurrection of the body" in the creeds. Jesus explains that the resurrection is unlike our current age altogether, but affirms that God is a God of the living not the dead. This foreshadows Jesus' own resurrection, which is the first fruits of our own resurrections (see 1 Corinthians 15:20).

Destruction of the Temple Foretold

Jesus predicts the destruction of the temple and then begins to speak of last things (eschatology). He tells of times of tribulation, hardship and persecution. But promises that we will be protected and through the trials we will gain our souls (21:17-19). Jesus foretells his second coming—the day of the Lord. He encourages his disciples to be alert, watching and waiting for it.

Discussion Questions:

1. In Jesus' triumphal entry there is a strange sense of irony. In what ways are we like the people that welcome him in only to turn on him later in the week?
2. As Christians, our citizenship of the kingdom of Heaven takes priority over any other citizenship or allegiance. Give some examples of when other allegiances conflict with Christian discipleship?
3. Research what it means to affirm the "resurrection of the dead" in the Apostles' Creed. Share it with the group.
4. In Jesus' life, death and resurrection the kingdom of God was inaugurated, but it does not come to completion until the "second coming" of Christ. How does the Second Coming strengthen Christians in our modern age of instant gratification?

Reflection: Read and reflect on the ancient Greek Hymn (Troparion) of the Feast of the Entry of the Lord into Jerusalem.

O Christ our God
When Thou didst raise Lazarus from the dead
before Thy Passion,
Thou didst confirm the resurrection of the universe.
Wherefore, we like children,
carry the banner of triumph and victory,
and we cry to Thee, O Conqueror of Death,
Hosanna in the highest!
Blessed is He that cometh in the Name of the Lord.

What do you think is meant by the "resurrection of the universe"? What does it mean for the church to "carry the banner of triumph and victory"?

Reflection 2: Compare Luke 21:25-28 with Daniel 7-14. Who is the Son of Man coming to in the texts? What phrases or images are repeated?

Closing Prayer:

Pray for any prayer requests. And invite members of the class to pray a prayer that is related to the scripture lesson. Close by saying the Apostles' Creed.

Notes

_____

_____

_____

_____

_____

_____

_____

_____

_____

_____

_____

_____

_____

_____

Notes

Lesson 7: The Passion and Resurrection

Objective: At the end of this session, the class will have understood some of the Lukan emphases in the passion and resurrection narratives and how these stories formulate Christian worship and Christian living.

Opening Prayer:

Almighty God, who through the death of your Son has destroyed sin and death, and by his resurrection has restored innocence and everlasting life, that we may be delivered from the dominion of the devil, and our mortal bodies raised up from the dead: grant that we may confidently and wholeheartedly believe this, and finally, with your saints, share in the joyful resurrection of the just; through the same Jesus Christ, your Son, our Lord.
     --Martin Luther

Reading: Luke 22:1-24:1-53

Lesson:

The Passion Narrative

Now Luke turns our attention to the climax of the gospel, the Passion narrative. These stories about Jesus were the most important to the early church and are thought to be the first stories to be written down about Jesus. Luke's telling of the Passion narrative is much more "orderly" than the other gospels. It is also interesting to note that it has many parallels to the Gospel of John and Pauline sources. The story starts with the chief priest plotting to kill Jesus. Jesus is in the last hours of his life, but his nature and ministry remain unchanged. While being arrested, he heals a man's ear. Even Jesus' presence causes reconciliation between Herod and Pilate (23:12). And while on the cross Jesus offers salvation to the thief (23:43). Jesus' ministry continues even in the most trying of circumstances.

The Lord's Supper

In Luke, the Last Supper is clearly a Passover meal. Jesus' passion is revealed against the backdrop of the slaughtered Passover lamb. There are two cups recorded in Luke as opposed to just one in the other synoptics. Passover was the feast of remembrance of Israel's salvation history. Jesus draws on those themes and the Eucharist becomes the chief feast of remembrance of salvation history for Christians.

> **Exercise:** For background on Passover read the *Learning Bible* description on p. 1932.

There is also a clear eschatological theme for the supper. It is a meal of the kingdom and a foretaste of the heavenly banquet to come. Luke's telling of the story closely resembles Paul's in 1 Corinthians 11. In it he veers from the Markan tradition to a more Pauline one. The Lord's Supper is the climax of the hospitality and feasting theme of the gospel. Jesus sets feasting as an ordinance and sacrament of the church.

The Betrayal and Arrest of Jesus

Jesus is handed over to the authorities by an ironic kiss from Judas. After the arrest, the disciples deny him and do not defend his case. Even Peter, who was the first to confess him as Messiah, denies him three times.

Jesus before the Powerful

Jesus then goes before the powerful leaders on trial. Pilate asks Jesus, "Are you the King of the Jews?" Jesus responds, "If you say so." There is great irony as Jesus the King of Jews and the whole world goes before the world's political leaders. Pilate gives the people a choice of two prisoners to release, and the people choose Barabbas. Even at the end of his life, his ministry is still about "release of the captives" from the Jubilee theme. Jesus takes the place of a murderer and insurrectionist on the cross.

The Crucifixion, Death, and Burial

In Luke, Jesus is surrounded by three parties of supporters: Simon the Cyrenian, a large multitude of people, and the women of Galilee. While being crucified Luke records three parties that mock him: the rulers, the soldiers, and another of the crucified. However, these mockings are mitigated by the acceptance of Jesus by three other parties: the Roman centurion, the sorrowful crowds, and the women followers. These three sets of three are a literary tool to highlight the people's reaction to Jesus' death. It would have been a great surprise to those hearing the gospel for the first time that this Jesus who is the Messiah and the Son of God actually dies. This has been a great stumbling block for many, but his death sits at the very center of the gospel. Christianity is a cross centered faith.

The Resurrection

The story does not end in death. Jesus is found to be risen from the dead. The tomb is empty, and the world has never been the same. Like the birth narrative an angel delivers the message by asking, "Why do you search for the living among the dead?" The resurrection is discovered first by women who play a major role in the gospel.

Exercise: To review other post-resurrection appearances see the Table on p. 1771 of the *TNIV Study Bible*.

After the Resurrection is the seemingly random appearance of Jesus on the road to Emmaus. It is fitting that Jesus appears to people on a journey because so much of Luke's gospel happens on the road. There is no other historical reference to the town of Emmaus or to Cleopas. To tell this story Luke breaks from his normal orderly account and timeline as if to proclaim that the risen Christ could have and does appear everywhere that the Word is proclaimed and the bread is broken (Eucharist). These disciples did not recognize Jesus until he broke the bread.

After this appearance, Jesus appears to the disciples. They were afraid that he was a ghost, but Jesus offers for them to touch him. His resurrection is physical and spiritual. Jesus even eats a piece of fish to prove it to them. Jesus then teaches them about the Scriptures (the Law of Moses, the Prophets, and the Psalms). He also commissions them to do the work of the gospel. Matthew's Great Commission is much better known, but Luke's gospel contains just as profound a commission. Disciples of Jesus are to go out to all nations proclaiming repentance and forgiveness. The church is to spread the gospel with its Jubilee theme of forgiveness around the world. This commission is to be done in the power of the Holy Spirit. Luke is already preparing readers for the main theme in his second volume, the Acts of the Apostles.

In Matthew's commission text the command is to "go". But in Luke Jesus says "stay". The disciples are to wait for the power of the Holy Spirit to come upon them before they "go into all the world." The work that Jesus calls them to is only possible with the power of the Spirit.

The Gospel ends with Jesus ascending into heaven. He blessed them and, they worshiped him. Only God is worthy of worship. They return to the temple where Luke's gospel began, to continue to bless God.

Discussion Questions:

1. What does it mean for the church to have the cross at the center of its faith? What does it mean for you to have the cross at the center of your life?
2. The resurrected Christ is with us every time we gather for worship and break bread together. Recount an experience when your "eyes were opened" and you experienced his presence.
3. The Holy Spirit empowers us to bring the gospel to all the nations teaching repentance and forgiveness. How is God calling you to proclaim his gospel?
4. Humanity's purpose is to worship God, how has reading and studying Luke's gospel changed the way that you worship?

Reflection:

 To the left is the San Damiano Cross. St. Francis of Assisi was standing before this cross when he heard the crucified Christ speak to him, "rebuild my church." What do you think Jesus is saying to the church today?

Reflection:

Karl Barth describes the Resurrection like no one else.

"In the Resurrection the new world of the Holy Spirit touches the old world of the flesh, but touches it as a tangent touches a circle, that is without touching it. ...The Resurrection is therefore an occurrence in history, which took place outside the gates of Jerusalem in the year A.D. 30, inasmuch as it there 'came to pass', was discovered and recognized. But inasmuch as the occurrence was conditioned by the Resurrection, in so far, that is, as it was not the 'coming to pass', or the discovery, or the recognition, which conditioned its necessity and appearance and revelation, the Resurrection is not an event in history at all."

What do you think he intends to convey?

Closing Prayer:

Have your pastor lead you in a service of Holy Communion or celebrate a Love Feast. Focus on the meal as a meal of remembrance of the Lord's passion as well as a feast of Christ's resurrection.

Notes

_____

_____

_____

_____

_____

_____

_____

_____

_____

_____

_____

_____

_____

Notes

_____

_____

_____

_____

_____

_____

_____

_____

_____

_____

_____

_____

_____

_____

Bibliography

Bauer, Walter, Edited by Frederick Danker. *A Greek Lexicon of the New Testament and other early Christian Literature.* Chicago: The University of Chicago Press, 1979.

Brown, Raymond E. *An Introduction to the New Testament.* New York: Double Day, 1997.

Craddock, Fred. *Interpretation Series: Luke.* (Louisville, KY: John Knox Press, 1990).

Culpepper, R. Alan. *Luke. New Interpreter's Bible Vol IX.* Nashville, TN: Abingdon Press, 1995.

Dana, H. E. & Julius Mantey. *A Manual Grammar of the Greek New Testament.* (Upper Saddle River, new Jersey: Prentice Hall, 1927.

Fitzmyer, Joseph A., S. J. *Luke X-XXIV. The Anchor Bible.* (New York: Bantam Doubleday Dell Publishing Group, Inc., 1985).

Jeremias, Joachim. *The Eucharist Words of Jesus,* trans. Norman Perrin. Philadelphia: Fortress, 1966.

Johnson, Luke Timothy. *Sacra Pagina: Luke.* Collegeville, MI: The Liturgical Press, 1991.

LaVerdiere, Eugene. *The Eucharist in Luke's Gospel.* Archdiocese of Chicago: Liturgy Training Publications, 1994.

Metzger, Bruce. *A Textual Commentary on the Greek New Testament.* (Germany: Biblia-Druck, D-Stuttgart, 1994).

Metzger, Bruce. *The Text of the New Testament.* (New York, Oxford University Press, 1992), 41-42.

The Harper Collins Study Bible, NRSV. New York: Harper Collins, 1993.

The Learning Bible (CEV). New York: American Bible Society, 2000.

Today's New International Version Study Bible. Grand Rapids, MI: Zondervan, 2006.

The New Interpreter's Study Bible. Nashville: Abingdon Press, 2003.

Notes

_____

_____

_____

_____

_____

_____

_____

_____

_____

_____

_____

_____

_____

_____

Appendix A: Participatory Study Method

How can I get more from my Bible reading?

There is no shortcut in Bible study. If you want to find what God has for you in scripture you will have to dig. There are some things you can do to make your study time more profitable. This brochure outlines an approach to Bible study which can help you both with devotional reading and with deeper study.

Preparation

Gather Materials — have pen, paper, highlighters or other markers and all materials you will need for study available.

Conditions — Find a place where you can study. If you study well with music playing, put some on. If you prefer quiet, arrange for a quiet place.

Resources — Get a small, well-selected set of study materials. For suggestions see the back panel.

Prayer

Pray specifically for an open mind to understand, an open heart to receive, enabling grace for the actions you will need to take.

Claim these promises:

> But if we confess our sins to God, he can always be trusted to forgive us and take our sins away.

(1 John 1:9)

I will sprinkle you with clean water, and you will be
clean and acceptable to me.   I will wash away
everything   that makes you unclean, and I will
remove your disgusting idols. I will take away your
stubborn heart and give you a new heart and a desire
to be faithful.   You will have only pure thoughts,
because I will put my Spirit in you and make you
eager to obey my laws and teachings.

(Ezekiel 36:25-27)

Get an Overview of the Passage

Read the passage multiple times. I use 12 or more, but any
number from 3 times up will help.

Memorizing is useful, at least of key texts. (This will also
require you to select key texts.) Read from different Bible
versions, to help you with your concentration and to open up
different ways of understanding the passage.

At this point don't use commentaries, study notes, your
concordance, anything which takes your concentration off of
the passage you are studying.

Study the Background

Find out who wrote the passage, to whom it was   written,
what is the situation being addressed, and what type of literature
it is.

Meditate, Question, Research, Compare
(Repeat as needed)

Meditate on the passage.   If you are having difficulty
meditating, think about telling someone else about the passage,

such as a friend in need of encouragement, someone who is unsaved, or a child. Think: What questions might they ask about this passage? You can formulate thought questions or fact questions. Fact questions are about what the author is actually saying. Thought questions may lead you to other revelations well beyond the intended statement of the passage.

You can use outlining at this stage, comparison to other scriptures, to writers in church history, or to current experience. Ask: What similar experience are we having today? Can this help me understand the passage. For example, if you have had a vision will that help you understand Ezekiel's vision in Ezekiel 1? Ask your friends about experiences they have had.

Some historical writers you might consult include Jerome, Aquinas, Augustine, Martin Luther, John Wesley, John Calvin, Charles Spurgeon and many, many others.

Share your Thoughts

Ask yourself how this has applied in your experience. Get to know the person you are sharing with. Share your experience and then the text. Always work from your own personal experience with God.

Store up the experiences your friends share with you to use in studying further scripture.

The purpose of sharing is not just to help others with your own insight. It is also intended to provide a check on what you think you have learned. It is easy to get off track in independent Bible study. Sharing helps keep you part of the community.

Make sure that some of your sharing is with people who have experience and training in study. Training and degrees does not guarantee accuracy, but it does provide a valuable check.

Example Passage

1 Kings 19:11-18

1.   Begin your study with prayer.

2.   Read the passage several times. Can you tell this story in your own words?

   a) Read 1 Kings 17-19. Check a Bible Handbook or study Bible for the background of 1 Kings.
   b) Consider how Elijah feels through this experience.
   c) Consider what God is trying to accomplish by giving Elijah these experiences.
   d) How did Elijah know the Lord was not in the wind, the earthquake or the fire?
   e) Can the Lord appear in such violent events? (Use your concordance, looking up wind, fire, and earthquake.)
   f) Does God respond to Elijah's complaint?   (Only indirectly; he gives him a task.)
   g) Is Elijah as much alone as he feels he is? (No, there are 7,000 more faithful people, v. 18.)
   h) What other Bible characters have experienced something similar to this? (Daniel 3—the fiery furnace.)
   i) What people in church history may have experienced something similar to this? (Any martyr or person who has suffered persecution.)
   j) Have you experienced similar feelings? Have you ever felt completely alone in your faith?

3.   Share your experiences!!

Example Prayer for Bible Study

Lord, take from me any thought habits which will keep me from hearing. Make me open to your voice and your voice alone.

Lord, help me to accept your people as my brothers and sisters in your kingdom let me learn and grow from both their weaknesses and their strengths.

Lord, I trust you to reveal yourself to your people the way you know is best. Let your will be done.

Lord, let me not only recognize but obey your voice. Let my actions be conformed to your will. Help me to love my neighbor as myself.

In Jesus' name, Amen.

Notes

_____

_____

_____

_____

_____

_____

_____

_____

_____

_____

_____

_____

_____

_____

Appendix B: Tools for Bible Study

The following are some suggested resources for Bible study. They fall into 7 categories:

Bible Versions

You will need a Bible version that you can understand without having to consult an English dictionary too often.

- ✔ For quick reading (overview):
    - ○ Contemporary English Version (CEV)
      3rd or 4th grade reading level; high degree of accuracy within the context of its aim for easy readability.
    - ○ The Message
      Heavily paraphrased with cultural terms translated. This version is fun to read, but will tend to obscure elements of the original cultures.
    - ○ New Living Translation (NLT)
      A more accurate revision of the Living Bible. This is the easy-reading Bible for evangelical Christians.
    - ○ Today's New International Version
      Shows its relationship to the popular NIV in many wordings, but uses simplified language and sentence structure in many cases.
- ✔ For study or reading:
    - ○ New International Version (NIV)
      The always popular NIV is the Bible of choice for evangelical Christians.
    - ○ Revised English Bible (REB)
      This version was translated by an inter-denominational committee with interfaith review. It contains some British English which may be hard on American ears.
- ✔ For study:

- ○ New Revised Standard Version (NRSV)
  The Bible of choice for mainline Christians needing a study Bible. The NRSV is often criticized for gender neutral language. It has also received interfaith review.
- ○ New American Standard Bible (NASB)
  An alternative to the NRSV that is more conservative in its renderings. It is also often a bit less readable. Very literal.
- ○ New King James Version (NKJV)
  Aimed primarily at fundamentalist and conservative Christians who prefer the manuscripts and text behind the KJV, but prefer updated English. Very literal and often a bit clumsy to read. Includes such disputed passages as Mark 16:9-20, John 7:53-8:11 and 1 John 5:7 & 8 which no other modern version includes.

Study Bibles

Study Bibles usually contain introductory articles giving Bible backgrounds, information on methodology and overviews of various themes in the Bible. They will also include introductions to each book and comments on difficult passages.

Study Bibles will reflect religious views of editors and authors, some more than others. Care should be taken to distinguish the Biblical text from the comments, and facts and opinions within the comments.

- ✔ Oxford Study Bible (REB)
  New Oxford Annotated Bible (NRSV)
  HarperCollins Study Bible (NRSV)
  Mainstream or liberal notes with acknowledgment of more conservative options (see definition of terms at the

end of this appendix). None of these labels are intended pejoratively.

✔ The NIV Study Bible (Zondervan)
  Evangelical study notes.

✔ Spirit Filled Life Bible
  Aimed at a more charismatic audience.

✔ Scofield Reference Bible (various editions and versions)
  A famous dispensational study Bible, commonly accepted amongst fundamentalists and many conservative Christians.

✔ Ryrie Study Bible (various editions and versions)
  Another well-loved conservative study Bible.

Bible Handbooks

Bible handbooks provide historical and cultural information, usually with a number of general articles and then comments on particular books and passages. Using a Bible handbook along with your Bible is like having a Bible with study notes, though usually having a handbook in a separate volume will mean that the handbook contains more exhaustive information.

Bible handbooks, like study Bibles, will reflect religious presuppositions of the editors. Use them carefully.

✔ Mainstream and/or Liberal
  The Cambridge Companion to the Bible

✔ Moderate/Conservative
  Eerdman's Handbook to the Bible
  Zondervan's Handbook to the Bible

✔ Conservative
  Halley's Bible Handbook

Background Documents

✔ Pritchard, Ancient Near Eastern Texts

Large, expensive, hard cover but a tremendous resource
for the Bible student.

✔ Pritchard, The Ancient Near East, Volume 1, An
Anthology   of   Texts   and   Pictures
(Both 1958 and 1975 editions still available)

✔ Charlesworth, James H. The Old Testament
Pseudepigrapha   (2   volumes).
This work is a standard for editions of these extra-
Biblical works.

Concordances

Concordances may be exhaustive, complete, or concise. Usage
of these terms is not 100% consistent. In addition they may
either be either organized by words or topics.

Many Bibles contain small, concise concordances. Many study
Bibles contain topical concordances.

Exhaustive concordances contain every reference to a word
listed under every word. Complete concordances contain
references to each and every verse, using significant terms,
though not necessarily under every word in the verse. Concise
concordances contain selective references and may not reference
all verses.

Concordances with Greek and/or Hebrew Lexicons can be
useful, but one should remember that translation is not so
simple as just picking a word from a dictionary definition. Such
concordances with lexicons are very often abused in discussions
about the Bible.

✔ Exhaustive with Greek/Hebrew
  ○ Goodrick and Kohlenberger, The NIV Exhaustive
    Concordance, Zondervan
  ○ Strong's Exhaustive Concordance.
    Based on the KJV and an older lexicon.

- ○ New American Standard Exhaustive Concordance of the Bible/Hebrew-Aramaic and Greek Dictionaries
- ○ New American Standard Strong's Exhaustive Concordance
- ✔ Exhaustive Concordances
- ○ NRSV Concordance Unabridged
- ✔ Complete Concordances
- ○ Cruden's Complete Concordance Concordance to the KJV.
- ✔ Concise Concordances
- ○ The Concise Concordance to the New Revised Standard Version (Oxford)
- ✔ Topical Concordances
- ○ Holman Concise Topical Concordance : An Easy to Use Alphabetical Reference Covering Hundreds of Topics (Holman Reference)

Bible Dictionaries

Bible Dictionaries provide definitions of various Biblical terms, information about places and people, and introductory information about Biblical books. Most information contained in a Bible handbook can be found in a Bible Dictionary but it will be organized much differently.

The religious views of authors and editors will impact the content of a Bible Dictionary.

- ✔ Mainstream
  - ○ HarperCollins Bible Dictionary
  - ○ Anchor Bible Dictionary (6 volumes)
  - ○ Interpreter's Dictionary of the Bible
- ✔ Evangelical
  - ○ New International Bible Dictionary

    ○ New Bible Dictionary (Intervarsity Press)

Bible Atlases

✔ Oxford Bible Atlas

✔ HarperCollins Concise Atlas of the Bible. Paperback and 152 pages, this one may be all the average Bible student needs!

✔ The Harper Atlas of World History

Some Definitions

Note: Labels in connection with many of these resources can be misleading. No label is to be regarded as either pejorative or complimentary. "Mainstream" doesn't mean "correct," for example.

Mainstream: Materials which would be suitable for use in departments of religion at secular universities. This does not imply more or less correct in content.

Interfaith: Involving persons other than those of one faith (Christians and Jews, for example). Distinguish from interdenominational.

Interdenominational: Involving persons from more than one Christian denomination. Distinguish from interfaith.

Only minimal bibliographical information is given in this appendix. It should be enough to locate materials in Books in Print or via online services such as Amazon.com or Barnes and Noble. For further information on resources, check the Participatory Bible Study web page, http://www.deepbiblestudy.com or http://lukestudy.com.

More from the Participatory Study Series:

To the Hebrews: A Participatory Study Guide

The book of Hebrews provides a unique view of the ministry of Jesus as Redeemer, priest, sacrifice, and king. This picture is presented as a call to endurance. Learn to live as a redeemed person through this powerful New Testament book, guided by a thematic study guide that invites you deeper into the book with each lesson. Includes 3, 8, and 13 lesson plans to accommodate everything from short studies to a Sunday School quarter.

Revelation: A Participatory Study Guide

Built around the metaphor of a theme park ride, inspired by The Pirates of the Caribbean, this study guide takes a visual approach to Revelation. It's not about dates and charts. It's not just about the future. It's about you and how you are going to live a Christian life in this world, but not of it.

Coming in the fall of 2009 ...

Learning and Living Scripture: A Guide to the Participatory Study Method

Henry Neufeld and Geoffrey Lentz, a teacher and a pastor, will team up to present this method of study in a practical, usable way. Learn to integrate prayer and scripture reading while also being faithful to the historical meaning of the text and its use throughout history by the community of faith.

This guide is not just about study and learning facts; it's about letting the God who gave scripture live in and through you as you learn and share.

To order, visit any major online retailer, or see our web site at:

EnergionDirect.com
http://www.energiondirect.com

Phone: (850) 525-3916
P. O. Box 841
Gonzalez, FL 32560

CPSIA information can be obtained at www.ICGtesting.com
Printed in the USA
LVOW12s2103100314

376789LV00002B/437/P